Sunday Coffee Date With Jesus

Psalm 143:8
Cause me to hear thy lovingkindness
in the morning; for in thee do I trust:
cause me to know the way
wherein I should walk;
for I lift up my soul unto thee.

Christian Journals
Engaging the Heart with the Word

Follow Us Online

ChristianJournals.org

fb.me/ChristianJournals1

twitter.com/ChristianJourn5

instagram.com/Christian_Journals

pinterest.com/ChristianJournals

this belongs to

To: Joni - Happy Birthday!
From your friend,
Bethany Pifer
2022

Date: / /

Topic

Speaker

Scripture References

Sermon Notes

_____
_____
_____
_____
_____
_____
_____
_____
_____
_____
_____
_____
_____
_____
_____
_____
_____
_____
_____
_____
_____
_____
_____

Questions or topics to research further

1. _____
2. _____
3. _____

One thing from the message to apply in my life

Just my thinking doodles

Prayer Requests / Announcements

_____
_____
_____
_____
_____
_____
_____
_____

Date: / /

Topic

Speaker

Scripture References

Sermon Notes

_____
_____
_____
_____
_____
_____
_____
_____
_____
_____
_____
_____
_____
_____
_____
_____
_____
_____
_____
_____
_____
_____
_____
_____
_____
_____
_____
_____
_____
_____

Questions or topics to research further

1. _____

2. _____

3. _____

One thing from the message to apply in my life

Just my thinking doodles

Prayer Requests / Announcements

_____
_____
_____
_____
_____
_____
_____
_____

Topic

Speaker

Scripture References

Sermon Notes

Questions or topics to research further

1. _____
2. _____
3. _____

One thing from the message to apply in my life

Just my thinking doodles

Prayer Requests / Announcements

_____
_____
_____
_____
_____
_____
_____
_____

Date: / /

Topic

Speaker

Scripture References

Sermon Notes

_____
_____
_____
_____
_____
_____
_____
_____
_____
_____
_____
_____
_____
_____
_____
_____
_____
_____
_____
_____
_____
_____
_____
_____
_____

Questions or topics to research further

1. _____
2. _____
3. _____

One thing from the message to apply in my life

Just my thinking doodles

Prayer Requests / Announcements

_____
_____
_____
_____
_____
_____
_____
_____

Date: / /

Topic

Speaker

Scripture References

Sermon Notes

_____
_____
_____
_____
_____
_____
_____
_____
_____
_____
_____
_____
_____
_____
_____
_____
_____
_____
_____
_____
_____
_____
_____
_____
_____
_____
_____
_____

Questions or topics to research further

1. _____
2. _____
3. _____

One thing from the message to apply in my life

Just my thinking doodles

Prayer Requests / Announcements

_____
_____
_____
_____
_____
_____
_____

Topic

Speaker

Scripture References

Sermon Notes

_____
_____
_____
_____
_____
_____
_____
_____
_____
_____
_____
_____
_____
_____
_____
_____
_____
_____
_____
_____
_____
_____
_____
_____
_____
_____
_____
_____

Questions or topics to research further

1. _____
2. _____
3. _____

One thing from the message to apply in my life

Just my thinking doodles

Prayer Requests / Announcements

_____
_____
_____
_____
_____
_____
_____
_____

Date: / /

Topic

Speaker

Scripture References

Sermon Notes

_____
_____
_____
_____
_____
_____
_____
_____
_____
_____
_____
_____
_____
_____
_____
_____
_____
_____
_____
_____
_____
_____
_____
_____
_____
_____
_____
_____
_____

Questions or topics to research further

1. _____
2. _____
3. _____

One thing from the message to apply in my life

Just my thinking doodles

Prayer Requests / Announcements

_____
_____
_____
_____
_____
_____
_____
_____

Topic

Speaker

Scripture References

Sermon Notes

_____
_____
_____
_____
_____
_____
_____
_____
_____
_____
_____
_____
_____
_____
_____
_____
_____
_____
_____
_____
_____
_____
_____
_____
_____

Questions or topics to research further

1. _____
2. _____
3. _____

One thing from the message to apply in my life

Just my thinking doodles

Prayer Requests / Announcements

_____
_____
_____
_____
_____
_____
_____
_____

Date: / /

Topic

Speaker

Scripture References

Sermon Notes

_____
_____
_____
_____
_____
_____
_____
_____
_____
_____
_____
_____
_____
_____
_____
_____
_____
_____
_____
_____
_____
_____
_____
_____
_____
_____
_____
_____

Questions or topics to research further

1. _____
2. _____
3. _____

One thing from the message to apply in my life

Just my thinking doodles

Prayer Requests / Announcements

_____
_____
_____
_____
_____
_____
_____
_____

Date: / /

Topic

Speaker

Scripture References

Sermon Notes

Questions or topics to research further

1. _____
2. _____
3. _____

...One thing from the message to apply in my life....

.... Just my thinking doodles ....

Prayer Requests / Announcements

_____
_____
_____
_____
_____
_____
_____

Topic

Speaker

Scripture References

Sermon Notes

_____
_____
_____
_____
_____
_____
_____
_____
_____
_____
_____
_____
_____
_____
_____
_____
_____
_____
_____
_____
_____
_____
_____
_____
_____
_____

Questions or topics to research further

1. _____
2. _____
3. _____

One thing from the message to apply in my life

Just my thinking doodles

Prayer Requests / Announcements

_____
_____
_____
_____
_____
_____
_____

Date: /   /

Topic

Speaker

Scripture References

Sermon Notes

_____
_____
_____
_____
_____
_____
_____
_____
_____
_____
_____
_____
_____
_____
_____
_____
_____
_____
_____
_____
_____
_____
_____
_____
_____
_____
_____
_____

Questions or topics to research further

1. _____
2. _____
3. _____

...One thing from the message to apply in my life....

.... Just my thinking doodles ....

Prayer Requests / Announcements

_____
_____
_____
_____
_____
_____
_____

Date: /   /

Topic

Speaker

Scripture References

Sermon Notes

_____
_____
_____
_____
_____
_____
_____
_____
_____
_____
_____
_____
_____
_____
_____
_____
_____
_____
_____
_____
_____
_____
_____
_____
_____
_____
_____
_____
_____

Questions or topics to research further

1. _____
2. _____
3. _____

···One thing from the message to apply in my life···

············ Just my thinking doodles ············

Prayer Requests / Announcements

_____
_____
_____
_____
_____
_____
_____

Date: /   /

Topic

Speaker

Scripture References

Sermon Notes

_____
_____
_____
_____
_____
_____
_____
_____
_____
_____
_____
_____
_____
_____
_____
_____
_____
_____
_____
_____
_____
_____
_____
_____
_____
_____
_____

Questions or topics to research further

1. _____
2. _____
3. _____

One thing from the message to apply in my life

Just my thinking doodles

Prayer Requests / Announcements

_____
_____
_____
_____
_____
_____
_____
_____

Date: / /

Topic

Speaker

Scripture References

Sermon Notes

_____
_____
_____
_____
_____
_____
_____
_____
_____
_____
_____
_____
_____
_____
_____
_____
_____
_____
_____
_____
_____
_____
_____
_____
_____
_____
_____
_____

Questions or topics to research further

1. _____
2. _____
3. _____

One thing from the message to apply in my life

Just my thinking doodles

Prayer Requests / Announcements

_____
_____
_____
_____
_____
_____
_____
_____

Date: / /

Topic

Speaker

Scripture References

Sermon Notes

Questions or topics to research further

1. _____
2. _____
3. _____

One thing from the message to apply in my life

Just my thinking doodles

Prayer Requests / Announcements

_____
_____
_____
_____
_____
_____
_____

Date: / /

Topic

Speaker

Scripture References

Sermon Notes

Questions or topics to research further

1. _____
2. _____
3. _____

···One thing from the message to apply in my life···

··········· Just my thinking doodles ···········

Prayer Requests / Announcements

_____
_____
_____
_____
_____
_____
_____

Date: / /

Topic

Speaker

Scripture References

Sermon Notes

_____
_____
_____
_____
_____
_____
_____
_____
_____
_____
_____
_____
_____
_____
_____
_____
_____
_____
_____
_____
_____
_____
_____
_____
_____
_____
_____
_____

Questions or topics to research further

1. _____

2. _____

3. _____

...One thing from the message to apply in my life...

Just my thinking doodles

Prayer Requests / Announcements

_____
_____
_____
_____
_____
_____
_____
_____

Date: / /

Topic

Speaker

Scripture References

Sermon Notes

_____
_____
_____
_____
_____
_____
_____
_____
_____
_____
_____
_____
_____
_____
_____
_____
_____
_____
_____
_____
_____
_____
_____
_____
_____
_____
_____
_____
_____

Questions or topics to research further

1. _____
2. _____
3. _____

One thing from the message to apply in my life

Just my thinking doodles

Prayer Requests / Announcements

_____
_____
_____
_____
_____
_____
_____
_____

Date: / /

Topic

Speaker

Scripture References

Sermon Notes

_____
_____
_____
_____
_____
_____
_____
_____
_____
_____
_____
_____
_____
_____
_____
_____
_____
_____
_____
_____
_____
_____
_____
_____
_____
_____

Questions or topics to research further

1. _____
2. _____
3. _____

One thing from the message to apply in my life

Just my thinking doodles

Prayer Requests / Announcements

_____
_____
_____
_____
_____
_____
_____
_____

Date: / /

Topic

Speaker

Scripture References

Sermon Notes

_____
_____
_____
_____
_____
_____
_____
_____
_____
_____
_____
_____
_____
_____
_____
_____
_____
_____
_____
_____
_____
_____
_____
_____
_____
_____

Questions or topics to research further

1. _____
2. _____
3. _____

...One thing from the message to apply in my life...

...Just my thinking doodles...

Prayer Requests / Announcements

_____
_____
_____
_____
_____
_____
_____
_____

Date: / /

Topic

Speaker

Scripture References

Sermon Notes

_____
_____
_____
_____
_____
_____
_____
_____
_____
_____
_____
_____
_____
_____
_____
_____
_____
_____
_____
_____
_____
_____
_____
_____
_____
_____
_____

Questions or topics to research further

1. _____
2. _____
3. _____

One thing from the message to apply in my life

Just my thinking doodles

Prayer Requests / Announcements

_____
_____
_____
_____
_____
_____
_____

Date: /   /

Topic

Speaker

Scripture References

Sermon Notes

_____
_____
_____
_____
_____
_____
_____
_____
_____
_____
_____
_____
_____
_____
_____
_____
_____
_____
_____
_____
_____
_____
_____
_____
_____
_____
_____
_____

Questions or topics to research further

1. _____
2. _____
3. _____

One thing from the message to apply in my life

Just my thinking doodles

Prayer Requests / Announcements

_____
_____
_____
_____
_____
_____
_____
_____

Topic

Speaker

Scripture References

Sermon Notes

_____
_____
_____
_____
_____
_____
_____
_____
_____
_____
_____
_____
_____
_____
_____
_____
_____
_____
_____
_____
_____
_____
_____
_____
_____
_____
_____
_____

Questions or topics to research further

1. _____
2. _____
3. _____

One thing from the message to apply in my life

Just my thinking doodles

Prayer Requests / Announcements

_____
_____
_____
_____
_____
_____
_____
_____

Date: / /

Topic

Speaker

Scripture References

Sermon Notes

_____
_____
_____
_____
_____
_____
_____
_____
_____
_____
_____
_____
_____
_____
_____
_____
_____
_____
_____
_____
_____
_____
_____
_____
_____
_____
_____

Questions or topics to research further

1. _____
2. _____
3. _____

One thing from the message to apply in my life

Just my thinking doodles

Prayer Requests / Announcements

_____
_____
_____
_____
_____
_____
_____
_____

Date: / /

Topic

Speaker

Scripture References

Sermon Notes

_____
_____
_____
_____
_____
_____
_____
_____
_____
_____
_____
_____
_____
_____
_____
_____
_____
_____
_____
_____
_____
_____
_____
_____
_____
_____
_____
_____

Questions or topics to research further

1. _____
2. _____
3. _____

One thing from the message to apply in my life

Just my thinking doodles

Prayer Requests / Announcements

_____
_____
_____
_____
_____
_____
_____

Date: /   /

Topic

Speaker

Scripture References

Sermon Notes

_____
_____
_____
_____
_____
_____
_____
_____
_____
_____
_____
_____
_____
_____
_____
_____
_____
_____
_____
_____
_____
_____
_____
_____

Questions or topics to research further

1. _____
2. _____
3. _____

...One thing from the message to apply in my life....

.... Just my thinking doodles ....

Prayer Requests / Announcements

_____
_____
_____
_____
_____
_____
_____

Date: /   /

Topic

Speaker

Scripture References

Sermon Notes

_____
_____
_____
_____
_____
_____
_____
_____
_____
_____
_____
_____
_____
_____
_____
_____
_____
_____
_____
_____
_____
_____
_____
_____
_____
_____
_____
_____
_____

Questions or topics to research further

1. _____
2. _____
3. _____

One thing from the message to apply in my life

Just my thinking doodles

Prayer Requests / Announcements

_____
_____
_____
_____
_____
_____
_____
_____

Topic

Speaker

Scripture References

Sermon Notes

_____
_____
_____
_____
_____
_____
_____
_____
_____
_____
_____
_____
_____
_____
_____
_____
_____
_____
_____
_____
_____
_____
_____
_____
_____
_____
_____

Questions or topics to research further

1. _____
2. _____
3. _____

One thing from the message to apply in my life

Just my thinking doodles

Prayer Requests / Announcements

_____
_____
_____
_____
_____
_____
_____
_____

Date: / /

Topic

Speaker

Scripture References

Sermon Notes

_____
_____
_____
_____
_____
_____
_____
_____
_____
_____
_____
_____
_____
_____
_____
_____
_____
_____
_____
_____
_____
_____
_____
_____
_____
_____

Questions or topics to research further

1. _____
2. _____
3. _____

One thing from the message to apply in my life

Just my thinking doodles

Prayer Requests / Announcements

_____
_____
_____
_____
_____
_____
_____
_____
_____

Topic

Speaker

Scripture References

Sermon Notes

_____
_____
_____
_____
_____
_____
_____
_____
_____
_____
_____
_____
_____
_____
_____
_____
_____
_____
_____
_____
_____
_____
_____
_____
_____

Questions or topics to research further

1. _____
2. _____
3. _____

One thing from the message to apply in my life

Just my thinking doodles

Prayer Requests / Announcements

_____
_____
_____
_____
_____
_____
_____
_____

Date: / /

Topic

Speaker

Scripture References

Sermon Notes

_____
_____
_____
_____
_____
_____
_____
_____
_____
_____
_____
_____
_____
_____
_____
_____
_____
_____
_____
_____
_____
_____
_____
_____
_____
_____
_____
_____
_____

Questions or topics to research further

1. _____
2. _____
3. _____

One thing from the message to apply in my life

Just my thinking doodles

Prayer Requests / Announcements

_____
_____
_____
_____
_____
_____
_____

Topic

Speaker

Scripture References

Sermon Notes

_____
_____
_____
_____
_____
_____
_____
_____
_____
_____
_____
_____
_____
_____
_____
_____
_____
_____
_____
_____
_____
_____
_____
_____

Questions or topics to research further

1. _____
2. _____
3. _____

One thing from the message to apply in my life...

Just my thinking doodles

Prayer Requests / Announcements

_____
_____
_____
_____
_____
_____
_____

Date: / /

Topic

Speaker

Scripture References

Sermon Notes

_____
_____
_____
_____
_____
_____
_____
_____
_____
_____
_____
_____
_____
_____
_____
_____
_____
_____
_____
_____
_____
_____
_____
_____
_____
_____
_____
_____
_____

Questions or topics to research further

1. _____
2. _____
3. _____

One thing from the message to apply in my life

Just my thinking doodles

Prayer Requests / Announcements

_____
_____
_____
_____
_____
_____
_____

Date: / /

Topic

Speaker

Scripture References

Sermon Notes

_____
_____
_____
_____
_____
_____
_____
_____
_____
_____
_____
_____
_____
_____
_____
_____
_____
_____
_____
_____
_____
_____
_____
_____
_____
_____
_____
_____
_____
_____

Questions or topics to research further

1. _____
2. _____
3. _____

One thing from the message to apply in my life

Just my thinking doodles

Prayer Requests / Announcements

_____
_____
_____
_____
_____
_____
_____
_____

Topic

Speaker

Scripture References

Sermon Notes

_____

_____

_____

_____

_____

_____

_____

_____

_____

_____

_____

_____

_____

_____

_____

_____

_____

_____

_____

_____

_____

_____

_____

_____

Questions or topics to research further

1. _____
2. _____
3. _____

One thing from the message to apply in my life

Just my thinking doodles

Prayer Requests / Announcements

_____
_____
_____
_____
_____
_____
_____
_____

Date: /   /

Topic

Speaker

Scripture References

Sermon Notes

_____
_____
_____
_____
_____
_____
_____
_____
_____
_____
_____
_____
_____
_____
_____
_____
_____
_____
_____
_____
_____
_____
_____
_____
_____
_____

Questions or topics to research further

1. _____
2. _____
3. _____

One thing from the message to apply in my life

Just my thinking doodles

Prayer Requests / Announcements

_____
_____
_____
_____
_____
_____
_____
_____

Topic

Speaker

Scripture References

Sermon Notes

_____
_____
_____
_____
_____
_____
_____
_____
_____
_____
_____
_____
_____
_____
_____
_____
_____
_____
_____
_____
_____
_____
_____
_____
_____

Questions or topics to research further

1. _____
2. _____
3. _____

One thing from the message to apply in my life

Just my thinking doodles

Prayer Requests / Announcements

_____
_____
_____
_____
_____
_____

Date: / /

Topic

Speaker

Scripture References

Sermon Notes

_____
_____
_____
_____
_____
_____
_____
_____
_____
_____
_____
_____
_____
_____
_____
_____
_____
_____
_____
_____
_____
_____
_____
_____
_____
_____
_____
_____

Questions or topics to research further

1. _____
2. _____
3. _____

One thing from the message to apply in my life

Just my thinking doodles

Prayer Requests / Announcements

_____
_____
_____
_____
_____
_____
_____
_____

Topic

Speaker

Scripture References

Sermon Notes

_____
_____
_____
_____
_____
_____
_____
_____
_____
_____
_____
_____
_____
_____
_____
_____
_____
_____
_____
_____
_____
_____
_____
_____
_____
_____

Questions or topics to research further

1.
2.
3.

One thing from the message to apply in my life

Just my thinking doodles

Prayer Requests / Announcements

Date: / /

Topic

Speaker

Scripture References

Sermon Notes

_____
_____
_____
_____
_____
_____
_____
_____
_____
_____
_____
_____
_____
_____
_____
_____
_____
_____
_____
_____
_____
_____
_____
_____
_____

Questions or topics to research further

1. _____
2. _____
3. _____

One thing from the message to apply in my life

Just my thinking doodles

Prayer Requests / Announcements

_____
_____
_____
_____
_____
_____
_____

Date: /   /

Topic

Speaker

Scripture References

Sermon Notes

_____
_____
_____
_____
_____
_____
_____
_____
_____
_____
_____
_____
_____
_____
_____
_____
_____
_____
_____
_____
_____
_____
_____
_____
_____
_____
_____

Questions or topics to research further

1. _____
2. _____
3. _____

One thing from the message to apply in my life

Just my thinking doodles

Prayer Requests / Announcements

_____
_____
_____
_____
_____
_____
_____
_____

Date: /   /

Topic

Speaker

Scripture References

Sermon Notes

Questions or topics to research further

1. _____
2. _____
3. _____

One thing from the message to apply in my life

Just my thinking doodles

Prayer Requests / Announcements

_____
_____
_____
_____
_____
_____
_____
_____

Date: /   /

Topic

Speaker

Scripture References

Sermon Notes

Questions or topics to research further

1. _____
2. _____
3. _____

One thing from the message to apply in my life

Just my thinking doodles

Prayer Requests / Announcements

_____
_____
_____
_____
_____
_____
_____
_____

Topic

Speaker

Scripture References

Sermon Notes

_____
_____
_____
_____
_____
_____
_____
_____
_____
_____
_____
_____
_____
_____
_____
_____
_____
_____
_____
_____
_____
_____
_____
_____
_____
_____
_____
_____

Questions or topics to research further

1. _____
2. _____
3. _____

One thing from the message to apply in my life

Just my thinking doodles

Prayer Requests / Announcements

_____
_____
_____
_____
_____
_____
_____
_____

Topic

Speaker

Scripture References

Sermon Notes

_____
_____
_____
_____
_____
_____
_____
_____
_____
_____
_____
_____
_____
_____
_____
_____
_____
_____
_____
_____
_____
_____
_____
_____
_____
_____
_____
_____

Questions or topics to research further

1. _____
2. _____
3. _____

··One thing from the message to apply in my life····

··········· Just my thinking doodles ············

Prayer Requests / Announcements

_____
_____
_____
_____
_____
_____
_____

Date: / /

Topic

Speaker

Scripture References

Sermon Notes

_____
_____
_____
_____
_____
_____
_____
_____
_____
_____
_____
_____
_____
_____
_____
_____
_____
_____
_____
_____
_____
_____
_____
_____
_____
_____
_____
_____

Questions or topics to research further

1. _____

2. _____

3. _____

One thing from the message to apply in my life

Just my thinking doodles

Prayer Requests / Announcements

_____
_____
_____
_____
_____
_____
_____
_____

Topic

Speaker

Scripture References

Sermon Notes

_____

_____

_____

_____

_____

_____

_____

_____

_____

_____

_____

_____

_____

_____

_____

_____

_____

_____

_____

_____

_____

_____

_____

_____

_____

_____

_____

Questions or topics to research further

1. _____
2. _____
3. _____

···One thing from the message to apply in my life····

···············Just my thinking doodles ···········

Prayer Requests / Announcements

_____
_____
_____
_____
_____
_____
_____
_____

Date: / /

Topic

Speaker

Scripture References

Sermon Notes

Questions or topics to research further

1. _____
2. _____
3. _____

One thing from the message to apply in my life

Just my thinking doodles

Prayer Requests / Announcements

_____
_____
_____
_____
_____
_____
_____

Date: / /

Topic

Speaker

Scripture References

Sermon Notes

_____

_____

_____

_____

_____

_____

_____

_____

_____

_____

_____

_____

_____

_____

_____

_____

_____

_____

_____

_____

_____

_____

_____

_____

_____

_____

Questions or topics to research further

1. _____
2. _____
3. _____

One thing from the message to apply in my life

Just my thinking doodles

Prayer Requests / Announcements

_____
_____
_____
_____
_____
_____
_____

Date: / /

Topic

Speaker

Scripture References

Sermon Notes

_____
_____
_____
_____
_____
_____
_____
_____
_____
_____
_____
_____
_____
_____
_____
_____
_____
_____
_____
_____
_____
_____
_____
_____
_____
_____
_____

Questions or topics to research further

1. _____
2. _____
3. _____

One thing from the message to apply in my life

Just my thinking doodles

Prayer Requests / Announcements

_____
_____
_____
_____
_____
_____
_____
_____
_____

Date: / /

Topic

Speaker

Scripture References

Sermon Notes

Questions or topics to research further

1. _____
2. _____
3. _____

One thing from the message to apply in my life

Just my thinking doodles

Prayer Requests / Announcements

_____
_____
_____
_____
_____
_____
_____
_____

Check Out Our Journals for Kids

www.ChristianJournals.org

Made in the USA
Las Vegas, NV
13 February 2022

43888417R00069